GET ER DONE

THE GREEN BERET GUIDE
TO PRODUCTIVITY

GET ER DONE

**THE GREEN BERET GUIDE
TO PRODUCTIVITY**

MICHAEL MARTEL

NEXT CENTURY
PUBLISHING

Get Er Done – The Green Beret Guide to Productivity

© 2014 by Michael Martel

Published by Next Century Publishing
www.nextcenturypublishing.com

Printed in the United States of America

HOW TO ORDER:

www.mikemartel.com

DEDICATION

This book is dedicated to my wife, who had to miss holidays, birthdays, and other important events with me because I was off at a training event or on some other adventure. She was, is, and will forever be my best friend. Her unwavering support has been the most important element in my ability to "get er done."

GET ER
DONE

THE GREEN BERET GUIDE
TO PRODUCTIVITY

FOREWORD

What a great read! Michael does a great job of putting his years of Green Beret training and military skills into real-life practical how-to's for succeeding in life. He translates the highly effective and intense training of the U.S. Army Green Berets and applies it to everyday civilian steps and systems to help people achieve their dreams.

This book lays out systematic and applicable steps to help people train for personal and business success. Michael weaves into *Get Er Done* the mindset and training techniques of one of the most prolific U.S.

military units in the world. Proficiency in any profession is determined by leadership, establishment of key confidence targets, and reduction of distractions to a minimum.

By assembling a mastermind or A-team, as Michael likes to call it, your mission, should you decide to accept it, is to commit to and achieve whatever goals and dreams are important to you and your family. Life is all about choices, and NOW is the time for you to organize your life, take a time-out to review where your point A is, and achieve what's next for you. Simply apply what you read in this book, put together a plan, see the BIG picture, and start producing the results you want.

So get your intention clear, take ACTION today, and complete the exercises at the end of each chapter. Then attack what's important to you, don't quit, and produce the results that align with your vision.

To your success!

FOREWORD

Tom Haupt

Leadership Expert, Motivational Speaker, and Best-selling Author of *TIME-OUT! Winning Strategies for Playing a Bigger Game in Life*

Get Er Done

TABLE OF CONTENTS

Get Er Done

INTRODUCTION

Why am I writing a book on getting things done? Throughout my career in both the corporate world and in public service, I have heard over and over again the complaint that the boss has given out an impossible task—that it just couldn't be done. Most of the time, the person given the task didn't even attempt to get started, having already decided that it was not within his or her ability to finish it.

You hear the same thing from family and friends. There is just too much to do. Or they say that there is no way they can do something different, something more challenging.

I was brought up differently. I am not taking about my childhood or how my primary and secondary education gave me the skills to go out in the world, although I believe I was raised to be accountable-- with a few detours here and there based on youthful indiscretion.

What I am talking about was my selection, training, and development as a Special Forces Green Beret. "Impossible" was not part of our vocabulary. We were expected to "get er done." This isn't to say that we were required to give our lives to make sure the trash got taken out. The means were always to be appropriate to the task. However, giving our lives was part of the equation when it came to protecting our country and the duties that came with it.

Get er done was simply a way of life. One of Special Forces' mottos is "Improvise, adapt, overcome." The concept is that we would take the situation as it was; there wasn't time or energy to waste on bemoaning what it should be. We would then take the skills that we had, could learn very quickly, or could purchase, and get er done.

The end result was, most often, success. The process might not follow the original plan, but because we approached things with the mindset of success, we stacked the deck and found the resources to make it happen.

During Operation Provide Comfort, thousands of Iraqi Kurds had fled Iraq into Turkey after Desert Storm because Saddam Hussein was waging a war of retaliation for their assistance to the coalition. The Kurds were stretched across Northern Iraq and Turkey. It was a humanitarian mess. My Special Forces Operational Detachment Alpha (ODA) had been inserted into Northern Iraq to help with the humanitarian effort to get the Kurds to move back into Iraq and the big United Nations' camps that had been established for them.

When the families fled, they took everything with them. This included the family automobile. We found abandoned cars stretched for miles leading up into the mountains that formed the border between Iraq and Turkey. Higher command decided that one way to get the Kurds to start moving back was to fuel up the cars so that they could be driven back down to the refugee camps.

My fellow weapons sergeant and I had been given the role of finders. That meant we were supposed to go out and talk to the locals to determine what resources were available. We were told to figure out how to get the gasoline distributed. On the surface, the task seemed impossible. We were in the middle of the mountains with limited roads.

We improvised, adapted, and overcame. Using a translator, we asked the local Kurdish guerrilla band, called the Pesh Merga, if they knew of anything that could possibly hold gasoline.

Incredibly, one of the fighters had been in the next valley over where someone had driven a gasoline tanker truck until it ran out of gas. We immediately set out for it with a can of gas in hand.

There it stood, a tanker truck just like you would see on the interstates back in the U.S. . It also had a family of five living in the tank, taking shelter from the elements. We exchanged a UN survival tent we had to get the family to move and clean out the tank. With the small amount of gas we had, we were able to get the tanker over to our valley and prepared to accept more gas from a military tanker when it arrived the next day.

We improvised, found something that would work, adapted the plan from what we thought would originally work, and accomplished the mission. If you follow these principles and some others I will share, you will get amazing results and find you are performing at levels you never thought possible.

At the end of each chapter, I give you a mission, should decide to accept it. This mission includes a list of things you can put in action right now to reap positive results in getting things done. It is your choice whether you put them in practice. As we said many times on my Special Forces teams, "You made the choice to be here." You made the choice to read this book, and you can make the choice to get results or not.

BACKWARD PLANNING

I actually learned backward planning before I attended the Special Forces Qualification "Q" Course; I learned it in U.S. Army Ranger School. Ranger School is primarily a leadership course that uses patrolling in harsh conditions to duplicate the stresses of combat. Ranger School is very demanding, with a planned lack of food and sleep. While some might say that many attendees spend Ranger School in a daze of confusion, hunger, and fatigue, backward planning does not mean that you plan in a confused or awkward manner.

One of the biggest factors in whether or not you get

your task completed is effective time management. Without good time management, you will almost always fail. This was beat into our heads by the Ranger School Ranger Instructors (RIs). The RIs would continually ask us what time we needed to be on the target.

"Time on target" was the time at which we had to get er done. Everything else led up to that time. We then mentally walked our way backward, putting time points at each important step. For example, if time on target was 2300 hours, then we needed to do a final reconnaissance of the target an hour beforehand. Given backward planning, our time there would be 2200 hours.

We had to set up a small patrol base in the area about fifteen minutes before then. This would be at 2145 hours. It would take us about three hours to get there from our present location. This meant that we would need to leave at 1845 hours. An hour to get our equipment ready, fifteen minutes to eat, and three hours planning meant that we would need to start getting ready at 1445 hours.

Backward planning lets you know when you need to get started. It also gives you timing points along the way to let you know if you need to adjust your plan in order to get er done when you need to. For example, if we ran late on the planning for the mission above, we might skip on eating or cut down on equipment prep time.

Think about how you could apply backward planning in your daily life. For example, the kids need to be picked up from school at 3:00 p.m. You need to get the dry cleaning, and the dry cleaners is fifteen minutes from the school. It will take you five minutes in the store. You therefore need to arrive at the dry cleaners at 2:40 p.m. Before that, you meet a friend at a local coffee shop. Half an hour for coffee. The shop is ten minutes from the dry cleaners. You need to arrive at the coffee shop at 2:00 p.m. Finally, the coffee shop is twenty minutes from your house. You need to leave home at 1:40 p.m. in order to do everything and pick up your kids on time.

Backward planning will serve you in anything that has a deadline or a time on target. In Special Forces, we were known for our focus on being on time. This kept us on track and on schedule. In combat, arriving too early might leave you exposed without air cover. Arriving too late at an ambush might mean that you missed your target. Either way resulted in failure.

It might be a good idea to think about this and why time management is so essential to success. Perhaps you can begin by thinking of the opposite—ways that do not work. Even if you have one very small task to complete, if you do not manage your time appropriately, it may get done too late or not at all. You may be working on a deadline or have a task that does not have a specific time to be completed. If you do not have a plan for getting it done on time, results will show that.

If you have ever felt that there are not enough hours in a day to do everything you need to do, this will be a very positive step for you. You will be pleasantly surprised with how much you can accomplish. With a game plan focused on mission completeness, you may find yourself getting more done each day than you usually accomplish in a week. Not only will you be more productive, but achieving each goal will come much easier. You will soon appreciate this all-important factor in your success.

Your Mission Should You Decide to Accept It:

- Take a several tasks you have to do today and conduct backward planning on each of them. Establish your final time on target, work backward, and decide when to start.

- If you use projects in your work, introduce the concept of backward planning. You will find that projects will have a much better chance of being completed on time.

REDUCING DISTRACTIONS

Distractions are killers. There are only a few other things that will prevent the mission, whatever it is, from being accomplished.

Concentration and focus are things that we as Green Berets made sure that we developed, practiced on a daily basis, and worked continually to improve.

Lack of concentration and focus could prove deadly. On a daily basis we worked with explosives. Lack of attention to detail could produce an electrical short that could set off the explosives. In other areas, lack of concentration could cause a parachute malfunction or a scuba-diving accident. Lack of detail in planning a mission could result in the loss of everyone involved.

So...obviously we put a high price on preventing distractions. One way we did this was by using the concept of isolation in mission planning. The Special Forces teams, upon receipt of a mission, would be kept away from other teams and anyone else not involved in the mission. They were escorted from their living quarters to the planning areas. Conversations with outside people were extremely limited. Exposure to newspapers, radios, and TVs was not allowed.

The idea was not to punish the team, but to create a focus that allowed ideas to be created without outside distractions. During this type of mission planning, we had very creative ideas that might have been diluted if we had permitted our thoughts to stray to other matters.

A non-military version of this would be what's

known as a "mastermind." Masterminds put like-minded people together to brainstorm ideas and hold each other accountable. During a mastermind session, you would not want outsiders distracting the meeting. The group's thoughts are focused on helping each member in turn accomplish his or her goal.

The idea of developing your own A-team is important. We need this synergy of thought that comes from like-minded people who are together and focused on a single purpose. You see this when men get together for fishing trips. The trip is not just about fishing; it is about being together as a group and talking about things in each other's lives with the power of the group.

In isolation mission planning, we didn't allow television, radio, or newspapers. We focused strictly on the planning for the upcoming mission. This kept our judgment from being swayed by outside influences. We relied on intelligence that had been verified and could be relied on.

Consider the distractions in your life. Reality TV, news, and other types of media are constantly invading our subconscious. I am not advocating segregating yourself from society, but implying that you should be judicious about what you allow to take up your time and your consciousness. Many people multitask, watching television and reading at the same time, but does that really do justice to either one? Why not concentrate on one thing and get the best results.

Your Mission Should You Decide to Accept It:

- Recognize that distractions are eating up the time in your life.

- Concentrate on one task at a time. Multitasking only creates multiple tasks that are completed in a halfway manner.

- Find a group you can be with to work on issues that affect you. It might be a pure mastermind group or something civic or spiritual in nature.

Get Er Done

JUST DON'T QUIT

I am going to let you in on a secret. Green Berets don't have superpowers; they are no different from the rest of the military or the civilian world. Most of them are not in Olympic-quality physical condition. Most are not on the academic level of a Rhodes Scholar. Overall, most are just like everyday people walking the street. But there is one big difference that I have found between the men I served with on A-teams and the rest of the world—they are not quitters.

The biggest existing qualifier for success is the ability to stay the course and continue on with what you have committed to. In any Special Forces career, there are many opportunities to quit along the way. In the beginning, quitting can be accomplished by simply raising a hand and self-selecting dismissal. In training, the nights are long, cold, and exhausting, and food is not plentiful. Trainees are expected to leave if they are not committed to sticking through the training. Better to leave at the beginning before a lot of money is spent training them...or, even worse, before they quit or try to quit before a live mission. The men who stay are not quitters. Much of Special Forces training and the work itself is an endurance event. You simply have to outlast whatever you are up against. The enemy is not the training; the enemy is your own mind telling you can't do complete your task.

This all translates back to your world. Most people give up way too early. The important things in life need time to develop, whether they may be a business, a career, or a marriage.

Your Mission Should You Decide to Accept It:

Simply don't quit. Take the time you need to develop success.

Get Er Done

MUSCLE MEMORY

I learned about the concept of muscle memory for shooting. One of my units had a special mission of Close Quarter Battle (CQB). CQB is basically what you see on TV when the SWAT team goes into a house to rescue hostages. We practiced the same type of close-in discriminating shooting for a military environment. You had to be dead-on accurate. Your life, your buddies' lives, and the lives of people you were rescuing depended on it.

Getting to a level of proficiency like this took time. We had to develop what is called muscle memory. Muscle memory occurs when your muscles perform a needed action without your consciously thinking it through. We would have to determine if someone was a threat and engage them with our rifle in a split second. If our rifle misfired, we carried pistols. We trained so that we could fire, transition to a pistol while moving, and hit the target within about a six-inch range in a couple of seconds. If you had to think about all of the movements necessary to accomplish this, it would take over a minute to complete the task.

Training for muscle memory starts out very slow. You break the movements down into segments. You raise the rifle, acquire the sights, and squeeze off a double tap (two rounds). If it malfunctions, you swing the rifle to the left with the left hand and the right hand goes to the pistol, draws it out of the holster, the thumb takes the safety off, and the left hand grasps the pistol at the middle of the body. You gently trigger squeeze to half cock, acquire the sights, and squeeze off two rounds. The standard for this sequence is under five seconds, all while moving and potentially under fire.

Muscle memory is developed by doing each of these steps very slowly until you have successfully performed them. Then you very incrementally speed up, adding the next step. If you make mistakes, you need to slow down. You only speed up and add steps when you reach perfection. We did not even use bullets to start out. We would dry fire (pretend to shoot an empty gun) until we were sure we were ready to move to the firing range. Once again, we would slow back down with the real bullets until we were dead on with our aim.

What we were doing was training the neurons in our bodies to react without conscious effort, sort of in the same way we breathe or even jump out of the way of a car without thinking about it. We just do it.

Now I know that most of you are not going to go into a house and save hostages. You are probably asking yourself, "Where does this muscle memory fit into my life?" It fits into everything. Muscle memory can be applied to both physical and mental activities. To help your sports game, you simply break the activity down into bite-sized chunks, practicing them until you get the movement down perfectly. Then slowly speed up, adding another movement. Slow down if you get out of rhythm.

Tennis is a good way to visualize this. You break the serve down into movements. Practice each part slowly until you get the movement perfect. Add another movement when you're ready. Finally, when you have the full serving movement complete, add the ball, keeping the serve very slow. Only when you are dead on with your serve should you speed up just a bit.

"Okay, so these Special Forces techniques are good for military and sports, but how do they translate into my life?" you ask. Simple—you have habits.

These habits were developed in the same way as muscle memory. You started off doing something slow and after a while you were doing it without even thinking of it. You can use muscle memory to create new habits and break habits you do not want to have. Simply start off slow, make sure you get the mechanics down, and then slowly speed up only when you are "dead-on."

Your Mission Should You Decide to Accept It:

- Find a task you want to get better at. Break it down into sequential steps.

- Practice each of the sequences until you can execute all of them flawlessly. If speed is a component, do it quicker and quicker.

- Keep adding sequences, only adding another when you can do the previous sequences perfectly. You will soon develop muscle memory and be able to perform the task more quickly and smoothly, and without thinking.

CONFIDENCE TARGETS

So what should you do first?

If you think back to when you were in school, you may remember teachers telling you that the best way to approach homework and other projects was to do the hardest task first. They may have also advised you to first tackle the homework subject you disliked the most, before moving on. I disagree. We used a different concept in what we called "confidence targets."

We used confidence targets when we taught combat skills to a group of soldiers. This could have been U.S. soldiers we were teaching ambush skills or it could have been soldiers from another country who we were teaching to blow up a bridge. The worst thing we could have done was pick the hardest, best-defended target for their first live mission. We always picked something easy to give them confidence. They had to know that they could do it—that they had it in them. After the first target, we would find others that progressively allowed them to practice their skills and get better without putting them in a situation they were not yet ready for.

This is easy to apply to your everyday life. Financial advisors commonly recommend paying off credit cards that have the highest interest payments first. While this makes sense, another strategy uses the confidence target method. In this technique, people should pay off the card with the lowest balance first. That way they see something accomplished. The next lowest card is then paid off. You see success building on success.

The confidence target method is a great way for children to build confidence in their abilities. Help them choose small goals that lead to bigger ones. If a child wants to sell cookies as a fundraiser, you do not immediately send them out into a strange neighborhood. Have them start out with family, then friends, and then neighbors you know. Each one of these steps builds their confidence before they strike out into unfamiliar territory.

If there is any common perception I have seen in people, it is lack of confidence in their abilities. By not having been properly trained and set up to boost confidence, they were set up for disappointment and disillusionment. Start out your children and students with confidence targets and you will see them be much more successful.

Train for Success

Another confidence booster that we used in the

Green Berets was that we trained for success. Training for success means that we did not expect failure. Don't get me wrong, we had contingency plan upon contingency plan in case something went wrong. We used the acronym PACE—Primary, Alternate, Contingency, Emergency. Each critical step of the mission had a PACE sequence. If the primary way in to a situation would not work, we went to the alternate, then to the contingency, and finally to the emergency. This was all done in planning, and we would rehearse and even drill each other on the different PACE variations for different parts of the mission.

"Failure is not an option" has become trite after its overuse in the media, but it was reality for us. First, what you think about has a way of becoming reality. We did not focus on what would happen if we did not succeed; we focused on making ourselves the best and on being best prepared to accomplish whatever the mission was.

We also trained to succeed. Every mission was rehearsed, sometimes *ad nauseam*. Even though we became sick of training and rehearsing, we always, always won in the end. When we cleared a building and rescued the hostages during training, we might get shot if we were using paintballs against real people acting as the bad guys. The Special Forces team members would never go down, even if hit by the paintballs. To do so would be to train our minds for failure. We would keep moving and finish the mission with the rest of the team. Later on, we would get a ribbing about the red paint marks on our uniforms and reflect on what we could have done better and how we could have avoided being shot.

We did this because it might give us a few more seconds in real combat. By training ourselves to instantly fall if shot by paintballs, we would have been training ourselves to instantly fall if shot in real life. It doesn't have to be that way. Many times you can continue to move after taking a round and perhaps eliminate the threat that put the bullet in you. To immediately lie down would be a death sentence.

What are you doing in your life where you immediately lie down when something doesn't go right? Train yourself to continue to drive on and finish what you started. If you practice expecting success and not lying down for failure, you will start seeing more and more successful moments.

Your Mission Should You Decide to Accept It:

- The next time you have to do something new, don't pick the hardest part as your starting point. Look for a confidence target to get yourself going.

- Start your children or teams out slow. Their confidence and ability will grow with each successful confidence target.

POINT OF NO RETURN

Once, we were standing in a field with the crew of an Air Force MC-130 Hercules. The C-130 is a Vietnam-era cargo aircraft that still gets heavy use carrying paratroopers and other type cargo. The M in front of the C-130 designates it as a member of the Special Operations Aviation branch. Special Ops MC-130s have additional avionics for flying at night and in-flight refueling, and other special capabilities.

The MC-130 has a large crew: two pilots, two navigators, an electronic warfare officer, a flight engineer, and two loadmasters. This contingent was standing in the middle of the field with my SF team, going through ambush drills with us. These guys were pure Air Force. They were used to being up in the air. They were not particularly thrilled with throwing themselves on the ground when the call "ambush right" or "ambush left" was sounded.

We ran through several drills and then went through the hand and arm signals our team used to communicate silently when we were on patrol in enemy territory. The crew took it seriously enough, but was happy to get it over with and be back in their warm flight quarters preparing for the upcoming mission.

You might be wondering why an Air Force crew was rehearsing overland movement with a Special Forces team. It had to do with the "point of no return." The rehearsals were part of a much bigger mission involving the blowing up of a strategic target—a bridge—deep in enemy territory. Our team was to infiltrate via parachute at night, move overland a significant distance, blow up the bridge, and then move to an extraction site to be taken out by Special Operations helicopters. If everything went according to plan, the last time we would see the MC-130 crew would be when we jumped out the door of their aircraft at about eight hundred feet above the ground over the drop zone.

However, things often didn't go as planned and we would have to make alternate plans. The point of no return comes into the equation here. MC-130s have all sorts of avionics that make them difficult to detect and shoot down. The crew was specially trained to disguise the profile of the plane, to fly extremely high and extremely low, and to use evasive maneuvers if detected…but sometimes that just wasn't good enough. The plane might be detected by radar and locked onto. It might meet an enemy combat air patrol. If the plane got hit before the point of no return, we would turn around and attempt to make it back to a friendly base. If we couldn't make it and had to bail, we would evade and try to be picked up by a search and rescue helicopter. Even though we were past the point of no return, we were committed. The idea was that we all would exit the aircraft, including the aircraft crew. Once on the ground, the Special Forces team leader would be in charge and take everyone on to accomplish the mission of blowing up the bridge. The Air Force crew had to be familiar with our movement techniques, combat drills, and signals if we were to have any chance of getting to the target without being detected. The idea of a point of no return was part of every mission-planning session. Once we were committed, we were going for it.

The idea of a point of no return is not new. Hernán Cortés, the Spanish conquistador who ended up bringing most of Mexico under the Spanish flag, used the same principle. When he landed in the New World with his men, he ordered their boats destroyed. Some accounts have him burning the boats while others have him ordering them scuttled or run aground. It doesn't matter how they destroyed the boats. The fact is that they had crossed the point of no return. The only way back home was to move forward and complete what they had set out to do.

It is all a matter of commitment. The point of no return gives us perspective on what we have committed to. During our mission, we knew that when the aircraft crossed a certain point on the map, we were committed. We were going for it. Everyone was in. Cortés also ensured that his men were committed. The only way back to civilization was for them to complete the mission. The only way back to their families and homes was to do what they had committed to do.

We make a lot of commitments in life. Marriage is one and having children is another. We make commitments to our spouses and children to do things for and with them. We make commitments to our employers to be on time at a certain place and to accomplish certain tasks.

We also make commitments to ourselves. We are going to eat right. We will work out. We are going to look for a better job. We make a commitment to find another source of income.

Why is it that you so often don't keep these commitments? Is it because you weren't committed enough? Is it because you did not make the effort to do what you said you were going to do? No, you were committed—just not to what you thought you were committed to.

When we took off on our mission in that aircraft, we were focused on the successful outcome of that mission. We focused on the result, in this case the blowing up of the bridge. Cortés and his men focused on the accumulation of riches for themselves and their superiors. In both cases, the focus was on what was about to happen.

If bad weather occurred or our mission ran into heavy anti-aircraft fire, those would be reasons why we could not continue. We could have focused on those. However, a commitment to reasons does not equate with results. A commitment to reasons makes us feel better and gives us cover if the plan does not work out as intended.

Things change. Your planning in life might not have taken all the possible hindrances into account. These hindrances are all reasons that can lead us to simply shelving our goal or our commitment. By focusing on the reasons, we are subjugating the results we said we wanted.

Too often we are committed to being reasonable. Reasons can be also called excuses. Many times in my military career, I was told that the commander did not want to hear excuses; he wanted to hear what happened. Note that I said "what happened" and not necessarily why things did not go a certain way.

Often there is another factor in our not completing our commitments. The fact is that most of us have competing commitments in our lives. A competing commitment is one that is directly opposed to our fulfilling our stated commitment.

Let's say that you have said that you will work out every morning in order to get in better shape, be healthier, and feel better physically. Why is it, then, that you continually forget to set the alarm and oversleep, thereby not having enough time to complete the workout?

The reason is a competing commitment. It could be a competing commitment to desiring more sleep. It could be a competing commitment to not wanting to feel sore after working out. It could be a competing commitment to being comfortable with the body shape you have already and not knowing what a potentially new figure might bring you. The theme here is that something is subconsciously driving you not to complete your stated commitment.

We had competing commitments by the dozen in the military. It was very easy to call off a mission for any number of reasons. We could say the weather was too extreme, we did not know enough about the situation, or we could use more training. I could go on *ad nauseam*. Were these the true reasons we had for canceling the mission? If we did not recognize the competing commitments we had—desire to be with our families, desire for comfort, fear of failure, fear of death—we could have fallen back onto reasons and cancelled the mission.

It is important to identify the competing commitments in your life. With every commitment you make, there is a choice not to do something else. Is this alternative going to show up as a competing commitment? Most likely it will. The key is to know this and be prepared for it.

First, when you make a commitment, understand what you are giving up in exchange for success. If you commit to helping your child with homework, you are giving up TV time, time out with friends, or time for yourself. Acknowledge that these could be competing commitments. By acknowledging them and bringing them out into the light, you have taken away most of their power.

If you are into the completion of your commitment and still not getting the results you expected, you need to examine what could be the competing commitments you have not identified. What are you doing and not doing to sabotage your results? Remember, in the end, it is the results that matter and not the reasons for why the results are not happening.

By focusing on results and not reasons, we keep in

mind what it is that we said we wanted. Your spouse, your children, your employer, and you yourself want what you said you would give them. You want the rewards that come from these results. Your needs and desires are important, just as you are. By staying result oriented, you keep that importance at the forefront.

Sometimes, when we still don't achieve the results we expected despite our efforts, it is because the effort really went into the competing commitment. Once we understand that, then we can redirect and get back on track. In Special Forces, we knew how easy it was to find reasons not to go out and train—commitments to comfort: too cold, too wet, too much time away from home. However, we kept in mind the results we wanted, being proficient in our chosen profession, and staying alive when our skills counted.

Your Mission Should You Decide to Accept It:

- List a commitment you have recently made.

- List the results you want to obtain from that commitment.

- List the competing commitments that you might have for that commitment.

Review this list daily to make sure you are not letting the competing commitments keep you away from your results.

BE A TRAINED OBSERVER

In one of my Special Forces units, we had a guy who we could dress up in the most ragged clothes and put on a park bench in any city in Europe. He looked like a homeless person and didn't get a second look from bystanders. He would mumble to himself constantly, and passersby would hear him speak in English, broken German, and a couple of other languages that he would mash together.

In reality, this guy was providing information back to our command center. He had an earpiece and a concealed microphone. He could lie in a dirty-looking sleeping bag on the bench and report information on a target we were observing.

Every Special Forces soldier is trained in observation. We had classes in sketching, report writing, and photography. The idea was that any one of us could be used to gather information.

We had men who were trained further in observation, our sniper-observers, such as the fellow on the bench. Sniper-Observers (S-Os) would normally cover a target, providing information on the target and the activity around it. Many times we would post an S-O team on each of the four sides of a building. The team would send back sketches of the building to include every sort of detail—the height and width of the doors and windows, the distance between them, the color of the building. They would provide sketched maps of the building's surroundings so we could make a hidden, silent approach.

The S-O teams would also report on the activity taking place around the target. We would get a call from one team on the north side, one looking out the window on the southeast corner, and so on. Many times these sessions would take place for three or four days, sometimes more and sometimes less.

What the teams were reporting was facts. They simply stated what they saw and nothing more. The interpretation then took place later with the intelligence analysts.

It was important that the information we received from our S-O teams was not cluttered with any implications attributed to it by a well-meaning team. For example, if the team was looking at only one side of the building, they might see a person exit the building and head around to the side where a car was parked. Then they would hear a car drive away. By putting meaning into this, they might assume that the person drove off in the car. However, they did not observe the person driving off. In reality, the person could have still been there and someone else who had already been in the car drove it away. This information—or misinformation—could be critical if an assault team was approaching the target from this direction.

We needed facts, not what the S-Os thought the meaning might be. The facts were simply what they saw, smelled, heard, or felt—basically what their senses reported to them. Those observations were what they were to report back to us.

In everyday life, we are exposed to millions of sensory inputs every minute. We have things that happen to us. We watch television and surf the Internet, where we are exposed to an increasing number of stimuli. These are all facts that are coming into us.

We have experiences that happen to us. The trouble begins when you attribute some sort of special meaning to these experiences and make them more than what they simply are. Let's say, for instance, that you are at your desk at work one morning. Your boss walks in, looks straight at you but does not say good morning to you, and walks quietly back to his office. There are a number meanings you could attribute to this. You might think that your boss is upset with you and might be close to firing you. You might think that the company is in trouble financially and might go under. The problem is that you are putting meaning to the boss's actions when you do not have all of the information. There could be an infinite number of reasons for why your boss did not acknowledge you. He could be preoccupied by something that happened at home. He could be mentally rehearsing a meeting that will occur later in the day. When we put meaning to something instead of relying on just the facts, we basically contaminate an honest appraisal of what is occurring.

We contaminate our view of the world by using beliefs about ourselves and applying them to the current situation. Many of these beliefs are common to everyone—worthiness, scarcity, the need to be right, fear of looking bad, fear of failure, and fear of rejection. Instead of plainly observing what is occurring, we take our fears and use our current experience to reinforce them.

When we take ourselves out of the moment and take on the role of a trained observer, we can simply realize that there is no meaning to the experience besides what we put on it. This is where the magic occurs. Let's say that instead of reacting to the non-speaking boss as a negative, we take it as an opportunity to reach out and give support.

Once you realize the power of being a trained observer, you can constantly reaffirm the positivity you want in your life.

The choice is yours. We can attribute negative meanings, reinforcing our fears and self-deceptions, or we can attribute positive meanings to events, thereby increasing our self-confidence and success. A trained observer understands what is happening and consciously chooses—to either attribute negative meanings or positive meaning to events— or to simply observe them.

Your Mission Should You Decide to Accept It:

- Take three events that you recently experienced. Write down each event as a trained observer, simply noting what happened.

- Write down what meaning you attributed to that experience at the time.

- Note why you wrote down this meaning. What kind of spin are you putting on the event? Is this a positive spin that will move you forward, or is it a subconscious negative spin that only reinforces your negative feelings?

Get Er Done

WHO ARE THEY TO JUDGE?

We had a lot of egos on our Special Forces team. Most of the guys were in top physical condition. On one team there was a guy who ran a sub-four-minute mile. On another team I had a team member who walked in off the street and won the U.S. Army's European heavyweight wrestling championship. With regard to intellect, I once had a team sergeant who had a photographic memory. He could look at or read anything once and have total recall. He had always been at the top of his class. Abilities like this were not unusual on Special Forces teams. Each one of our guys brought something special. We attracted people like this because of the mission and the training. The teams had some of America's best on them.

I often thought of the Special Forces A-team as a lot like a professional baseball team. All the guys had come up through the ranks or minors. Each was in very good physical condition and extremely good at what they did. We traveled together quite often and spent more time with each other than we did with our families. As with baseball teams, there was a lot of competition, ego, and personality in the team room or club house.

One of our ongoing sayings was "Who are they to judge us?" That basically meant that people outside Special Operations didn't realize the difficulty of our training and the resulting missions—that they did not have the perspective to be able to render sufficient judgment on our success or failure. That did not mean that we looked down on people outside our community, only that we were the best judges of ourselves.

And judge ourselves we did, oftentimes very critically. We frequently used what we called an After Action Review (AAR). During an AAR, we would foster an environment where we put aside competition, ego, and personality, and openly and honestly discussed what had happened in enough detail that everyone understood what did and did not occur and why, and what worked and did not work.

The idea was that not everyone would see everything. Even then, the portion of what we saw was tarnished by our perceptions and what we experienced. When we got everyone's point of view, we could truly understand all that happened or did not happen.

It is important to understand the concept of leadership in the military. A leader is responsible for all that happens and fails to happen with his unit.

This means that if they perform well, he is responsible, and if they perform poorly, he is responsible. This pure form of accountability puts the burden on the leader to make sure his team is ready to go. Special Forces teams take this even to a new level, since each man is senior and an expert in their area of responsibility; therefore, they are all leaders even if they don't carry the title of team sergeant or team leader. Each member of the team takes its successes and failures very personally.

After Action Reviews gave us the opportunity to get better. We used pretty much the same format with the idea of discussing what happened and exchanging ideas and observations, all with the goal of getting better. Basically, after every training we would conduct an AAR. It would be as simple as huddling up and going through the training event step by step. We always kept what we intended to achieve as the focus. We talked about everyone's individual performance, the performance of any specialty teams, and the overall performance of the group.

In an After Action Review, we didn't want to leave anything out. We didn't worry about hurt feelings, because hurt feelings won't get you killed in combat but being in the wrong position or not on time will.

Don't get me wrong though; AARs were not blame sessions. The focus was on determining strengths and weaknesses and finding ways to make the strengths stronger and to improve on the weaknesses.

You can use After Action Reviews in numerous places in your life. I like to use a daily AAR at the end of the day before I go to sleep. I review all that happened that particular day, good and bad. I look at what I did well and what sort of positive results I got. I also review what didn't go so well and the results that came out of that. You basically want to think about these questions: What was planned?

What really happened? Why did it happen? What can I do better next time?

You shouldn't over analyze the day's events. Short of a major catastrophe that really needs to be examined in depth, think about only the highlights and move on. This isn't about beating yourself up; it is about making yourself better.

The daily AAR can also be used in a business environment and put into practice after every shift. The shift supervisor simply gets the team together at the end of the shift and goes through the discussion: What was planned? What really happened? Why did it happen? What can we do better next time?

In the beginning, you should watch that you don't let the discussion fall into minutiae. Just get the team together immediately after the shift when everything is fresh in their minds and walk them through the four questions above.

For a business environment, compare performance against established expectations. Did we reach our daily sales goals? Did we produce an established level of whatever product we manufacture? If so, why? If not, why? Were there barriers present? What were they? How can we mitigate them in the future?

Finally, another occasion to use an AAR is after a big event or a project, or work toward a goal. You can conduct After Action Reviews at the end, although I would recommend setting milestones (milestones are check-in points during a project or a task that takes a while to accomplish) and conducting an AAR at each milestone to make whatever course corrections are necessary.

AARs can be conducted with basically any sort of unit that performs tasks. As I said before, you can conduct an AAR by yourself or with family, business teams, sports teams, civic groups, volunteer groups, etc. An After Action Review is your opportunity to capitalize on the observations of the group in order to perform better.

Let's hit the four questions to give you a blueprint to use for an After Action Review.

What was Planned?

What were our plans, goals, or objectives for what was to occur? Did we expect any barriers or opposition to our plan?

What Really Happened?

If you have time, have each person talk through what they perceived as occurring. You will find a lot of different perceptions of the actual event. Did everyone understand exactly what they were supposed to do? Did they understand what was happening around them?

As you talk about what happened, compare it to the

original plan. Were the obstacles we experienced what we expected? Were there unexpected obstacles? How did we respond to the obstacles?

Why Did It Happen?

Talk or think about what went successfully. We have a natural tendency to concentrate on what went wrong. It is equally or even more important to know what is effective and what works in order to use it again in the future. With your teams or family, reinforce activities, actions, and behaviors that got the results you desired.

With failures, concentrate on what should have happened and then on what didn't happen. You can certainly discuss it if someone should have done something but didn't, but blame should not be placed during an AAR.

What Can We Do Better Next Time?

Capitalize on your successes. If things didn't go as planned and you didn't perform as expected, think about how you can get training or practice. Perhaps you want to avoid that area in the future. When you are planning your next steps or next project or even looking to the next day, take what you want to improve on and add it into your plan.

****

We almost always did an After Action Review, no matter whether our mission was a training or a live mission. One point to keep in mind is a saying we had: "No high-fives on the OBJ." This basically translated into "Don't congratulate yourself until the mission is over and you are back at your friendly base." We could have been shot down in the process of flying back or something else could have always happened. With the exception of milestone AARs, don't do an AAR until all the steps are complete.

AARs helped us in many ways. It was a development process. Our junior team members got to see the big picture and learn from the experience of the more senior members. We were able to set better goals because we knew our strengths. We were able to plan training for the future to improve on our weaker areas. Finally, it helped us build cohesion in our unit by having common understandings and stories of our experiences.

You can have these same benefits with your teams, whether they are work, friend, or family related. You can also benefit by doing AARs by yourself to gain understanding and perspective of your daily activities.

Your Mission Should You Decide to Accept It:

- Conduct an AAR on your day's activities as you lie in bed tonight. Concentrate on your successes. Congratulate yourself on them. Think about what should have happened but didn't. Decide how you are going to make better goals and achieve them tomorrow.

- Start doing AARs with your family and work teams. You don't need to call them After Action Reviews. Just say that you want to review what just happened. Cover what was planned, what really happened, why it happened, and what can be done better next time.

COMMANDER'S INTENT

Back before I became a Green Beret, I was a paratrooper. The 82nd Airborne, an Army unit that has a history going back to World War II, is basically an army combat division that has the capability of inserting its soldiers via parachute onto the battlefield. It has its share of different subunits to include infantry, artillery, armored cavalry, and others. I was an infantryman and spent about three and half years in that position. About halfway into my time in the infantry, I became a jumpmaster and led many parachute jumps.

A typical parachute jump might consist of a combat

brigade with all of the necessary support units—perhaps a total of about two thousand people. The jump would be conducted at night. Paratroopers would fill cargo aircraft that would fly in lines, night sky would be filled with parachutes. After the paratroopers landed, they would have to collect their parachute and then move to an established linkup point with their unit. The night, of course, was not over. There was always a mission that followed. It could be a raid, an ambush, or just a blocking position in support of another unit.

The big parachute jumps of World War II were conducted much the same way. You might have heard of them—Sicily, Salerno, Normandy, Market Garden. All of these operations had to deal with poor weather, anti-aircraft fire, and poor navigation by the Air Force, plus the normal confusion of a parachute jump on top of that.

These conditions resulted in most of the

paratroopers landing in the wrong drop zone and not even making it to the battlefield. You had units missing most of their members and other groups that were mix-and-matched from soldiers that had been separated from their units.

You would think with this much chaos and confusion that the missions were doomed to fail. However, everyone knows that the Allies went on to take Europe with these operations being key victories.

The reason that these paratroopers were able to overcome the challenges was because they knew and understood the "commander's intent." Prior to every mission, the commander would put in simple terms what he needed accomplished for that mission. For example, "We will land and move north, destroying bridges along the way. Our intent is to deprive the enemy of the freedom of movement on the roads." The paratroopers, knowing this intent, could gather those around them, form small units, and still accomplish the mission. The operation might not go off exactly as planned, but the paratroopers were still able to make it work.

Commander's intent fully recognizes the fog of battle, the confusion that will inevitably occur, and the changes that cannot be anticipated. The goal is to give people the information they need to complete the plan and empower them, guiding their improvisation and initiative.

Modern-day paratroopers still have the commander's intent as part of their mission brief. We also used it in Special Forces. One of ours might have been something like, "Using speed, surprise, and violence of action, we will recover the hostages alive and unharmed, collecting whatever intelligence possible from the rescue site." By having a statement like this, I knew whether it was my job or not to collect a piece of information that I saw and bring it back to base.

You can use the idea of commander's intent in your life. As a parent, instead of telling your teens exactly how to do something, give them your intent. Give them the freedom to come up with their own way of accomplishing the task. Instead of taking the responsibility for success away from them, it puts the responsibility back on them. You will find them much more energetic and cooperative when you use the idea of intent.

The business world also benefits from the idea of commander's intent. Its reverse is micromanaging. Micromanaging is an innovation killer and will doom a task or project when the unexpected happens. The workers will simply stop and wait for direction. The problem is that you have only given them one course of action. When you give your intent and let them get it done, they have an unlimited set of action courses from which to choose. You will find them much more productive and able to adapt to change.

Commander's intent can help you in your own activities. Before starting a task or project, visualize what you want it to look like when you are done. This visualization will help you stay on course as you navigate whatever obstacles get in your way. You may have do things differently than you planned, but your intent will guide you toward your ultimate goal.

Instead of constructing a detailed plan for yourself and focusing on it, the vision from a commander's intent will cause you to make the right choices when the unexpected occurs. I am not saying that detailed planning is not important (as a Green Beret, we would plan for days and sometimes weeks for a mission), but at the same time, you need to be prepared to "adapt, improvise, and overcome."

The commander's intent is the clear description of

what success looks like. A good commander's intent allows people (and you) to adapt using inventiveness and resourcefulness to reach your goals.

Your Mission Should You Decide to Accept It:

- Next time you tell someone (your teen, a team member, etc.) that you need something done, instead of telling them how to do it, tell them what you want done and what it should look like when they're finished.

- Next time you take on a task yourself, visualize the end result. Hold that vision in your mind while performing the task.

Get Michael's other books on Amazon

www.amazon.com/author/michaelmartel

Get Er Done

ABOUT THE AUTHOR

Michael (Mike) Martel is a former Green Beret, a trainer, a teacher, and a leader. He focuses on helping people get started, make things happen, and enjoy success in life.

When Mike was barely eighteen years old, he walked into the Army recruiter's office in his hometown of Dayton, Ohio. He said he wanted to see the world. That wish was satisfied when he was shipped off to Berlin, Germany, where he had a great time in the "Divided City." There began his love of travel. He spent a total of thirteen years living in Germany and traveling around Europe, the Middle East, and Africa. His Army career spanned twenty years, including time as an infantryman, a paratrooper, and a Green Beret.

After retiring from the Army, Mike moved on to the technology sector, where he worked as a computer security expert, keeping extremely sensitive information safe from hackers. He earned a bachelor's degree in computer science in information technology and a master's degree in business management along the way.

Mike was quickly recognized for his leadership, knowledge, and ability to work with people. He moved into the executive ranks and led large business divisions.

Always on the lookout for a challenge, he discovered he had a gift for coaching. From his experiences, both in the military and in the corporate world, he has a lot to give back. His real-world leadership experience, combined with his technical education and skill, give him the unique ability to work with other leaders to help them achieve success.

He offers coaching to people, basically acting as an accountability partner. He helps them pick out BAGs (Big Audacious Goals) that they have always wanted to achieve. He then acts as their